MODERN NETWORK ARCHITECTURES NETWORK AND SYSTEM PROTECTION

- Understand what a computer network is

- To get acquainted with the types of networks and modern network architectures

- To study the components for creating a network

- Get acquainted with abstract concepts of networks such as the so-called "Internet of Things"

- To get acquainted with types of threats and measures for the protection of networks and systems

VLADIMIR VELINOV

Table of Contents

Introduction

In today's world, we are all constantly connected to other people, thanks to networks. We communicate with friends and partners in social networks and use the global computer network Internet for all kinds of tasks and purposes. A computer network is a set of two or more computer systems connected to exchange information or to perform some common work. Different types of computer networks have different purposes, sizes, and principles of construction. In addition to the global Internet, to which we connect our laptops, phones, tablets, and other devices daily to gather information, communicate with others, work, and have fun, there are computer networks in other places that we probably don't think about. For example, the individual important parts of our car are controlled by specialized computers, which are also connected to a network to exchange information. ATMs and POS devices from which we withdraw banknotes or pay bills also work thanks to a network that connects them to other devices, which determine whether each transaction will be approved or rejected according to the customer's condition. One of the main characteristics of a computer network is its speed and data transfer capacity. Speed and capacity are important because different applications have different speeds and capacity requirements. Every well-developed computer company needs a well-functioning computer network. Modern networks can include many components.

Both in the real world and in the virtual there are threats to its inhabitants or as explained in one of the experiments conducted by DefCon's Kevin Roose – "we all know that there are people who are masters of martial arts, and if they choose, there is nothing to stop them from attacking us, possibly beat us up, and there is nothing we can do right now. to stop them." The same applies to all of our electronic devices connected to the Internet, be they a laptop, smartphone, tablet or after the advent of the Internet of Things – even home appliances. There are people who are good enough to manipulate computer networks and systems, so if they decide to attack us, there's nothing we can do to prevent an attack, if we ever find out about it.

In any organization or private home, to a greater or lesser extent, people strive to achieve the security of their data, be it business data or photos they have taken over the past summer. At least once, each person has individually thought about what threats exist and are exploited, what vulnerabilities our devices hide, what is the chance that our device will fall under the blows of hackers. However, people rarely use terms such as vulnerability, threat, risk, etc. correct. Therefore, we will define them so that we get an idea of what is behind these names, starting with the assets.

Assets are everything that has value for the organization, its business operations, including the information resources on which its mission is based. The threat is any case, whether intentional or unintentional, that has the potential to harm the organization or person through denial of service, unauthorized access, destruction, alteration, or disclosure of information. The vulnerability is a weakness of the asset. Whether it is a factory defect in its production or an error in the implementation of this asset in a system, this weakness can lead to unwanted and unexpected compromising the security of computer systems, networks, applications, or protocols used. An exploit is a software code or a series of commands that take advantage of a specific vulnerability in a hardware or software computer system and cause unexpected or unwanted system behavior. Risk, in turn, is the potential of a threat to exploit a vulnerability in an asset or group of assets and cause harm to the organization or person holding the asset. In other words, the asset is what we are trying to protect, the threat is what we are trying to protect ourselves from, the vulnerability is the " hole" in our attempt to protect, and the risk is where the assets intersect, the threats and vulnerabilities.

Information security, and in particular the protection of computer systems and networks, is the part of information technology that has developed most rapidly and comprehensively in recent years. The topicality of the topic is recognized in all spheres of business and its research is the subject of interest of more and more modern scientific activities.

Relevance and motivation:

In today's world, every corporation, as well as all government organizations, collect, store, process and exchange information electronically through digital means or the Internet. In many cases, this information has the status of confidential or privileged information which makes it interesting for third parties. In the most general case, these individuals seek personal gain using this information. With the frequent use of information technology in all areas of business, the window for penetration by malicious individuals is growing, respectively, and the need to protect the perimeter, networks, systems, and information in them. Learned protection provisions and conventional methods work, but not well enough. To be able to qualitatively protect our assets, we need to know well the anatomy of the attack - what are the types, how they are carried out, etc.

The purpose of this book is to describe the most common attacks that threaten modern computer networks and systems, to describe the attack vector, as well as the most common vulnerabilities in these systems and networks. Methods and means that can be used for prevention and protection against malicious actions are considered. Modern good practices are also described for reducing the probability of a successful attack, as well as for limiting the damage in case of a successful one.

Tasks:

➢ Introduction and analysis of cyber-attacks against computer systems that have occurred in recent years;

➢ Description of methods for prevention of different types of attacks, complex protection;

➢ Indication of exemplary tools that can be implemented and used to ensure the confidentiality, integrity, and integrity of information;

➢ Description of the ways for implementation and application of already established good practices.

The object of this book is the study of some of the largest computer attacks undertaken to date, as an indication of possible protection measures that can be taken against such actions in the future.

The subject is seen as the material is to examine the vulnerabilities and exploits used to compromise computer systems and networks as well as methods for reducing the scale of the damage that attacks can inflict. Without adequate knowledge of the types of attacks, it is impossible to build a realistic idea of possible future ones and how to protect ourselves from them.

Methodology minutes include empirical methods

such as observation, comparison, and measurement, and some empirical and theoretical methods - analysis, synthesis, induction, deduction, verification. Primary theoretical information has been collected, the general and various aspects of the considered threats have been established, and the result is the search for generalized empirical facts. The study of the listed threats was carried out by segmenting the general concepts into separate components and subsequent merging of these components to establish the way of thinking of the attackers, as well as the vector of attack. The data obtained identify current problems related to cyberattacks, which helps to find appropriate solutions for them. On the other hand, these solutions can become the basis for a possible more sophisticated methodology for dealing with cyber attacks in the future.

CHAPTER I. NETWORK CONCEPTS, MODELS AND STANDARDS

1.1- Introduction

A computer network is a set of hardware components and computers connected through a transmission medium that allows the exchange of information between them. Devices involved in the network to exchange data must be connected through connection technology. The most common connections are cable (coaxial, twisted pair, or optical cable) and wireless (radio wave, satellite transmission, laser, or infrared technology). It is possible to connect via an additional device - router (router). The most famous network is the Internet. The transmission of data over the network is governed by special rules called network protocols. The Internet, for example, is based on a protocol called TCP / IP (Transmission Control Protocol / Internet Protocol). Years after computers appeared, a small number of them were connected to a network. They worked as small information islands, with no connection to each other. The data between the computers was transferred by copying it to a floppy disk, transferring that disk to the other computer, and copying the data to the target machine.

1.2- Network Categorizations

Categorization according to the roles of the individual computers

• Peer-to-peer networks

In peer-to-peer networks, each computer can provide services to others on the network, as well as use the services provided by other computers. Peer-to-peer networks are cheap to build and are designed for a small number of computers (according to Microsoft - up to 10). They usually have a user operating system, such as Windows or Linux, installed on each computer, and a user can run and run programs on it. Each user decides for himself what resources on his computer (disk space, printers) he will allow to be used by other computers in the network and what rights he will give to other users. The administration of this type of network is distributed - the names of users, their passwords, and rights are assigned separately on each computer and one user can have different passwords and rights on different computers. Peer-to-peer networks are suitable for a home environment where anyone can share photos, videos, and other documents with others, and anyone can print to a printer connected to one of the computers on the network.

• Server-based networks (client-server)

Server-based networks have one or more specialized computers, called servers, with a network operating system installed that supports network functions. If the server is down, there are usually no services available over the network for users' computers, or the network does not work. Therefore, servers are often located in a specialized room, without access to unauthorized persons. Usually, the servers do not employ users, and they are dedicated specifically to maintain the operation of the services, which makes this type of network more expensive than the previous ones. Sometimes network server operating systems can cost a lot. In server-based networks, the administration is centralized - all settings, usernames, passwords, rights, and other parameters are created and changed once only on the server and apply to the entire network, which increases the security of these solutions. Server-based networks are typical of medium and large offices and institutions, schools, universities, and other organizations with more computers and in need of greater network security and stability.

Categorization according to the services provided

- Internet access networks

These networks are usually built by organizations called Internet Service Providers (ISPs) and are designed to provide users with access to the resources of the World Wide Web - the Internet. Often in such networks, the service provider does not provide additional resources to users, but only allows them to access third-party such servers located somewhere on the Internet. Sometimes users of the same ISP cannot share services with each other, even though they are physically connected to the same network.

- Resource sharing networks

These are usually office computer networks in which a group of people shares common resources - files, printers, documents, whether these resources are located on a server, on local computers, or on a specialized work device. There may bent levels of access to determine which user can work with which resource.

Such networks often have access to the Internet, but network resources should only be available to employees within the network and additional measures should be taken to protect them from external users. Often Internet access in such networks may be limited to certain places or services.

- Corporate networks

The corporate network connects the individual offices and devices of an organization in a common network, so that all employees can exchange information with each other, regardless of which office and department they are located. In the corporate network, the protection from external access to the company's documents is given special attention. When connecting to remote offices, WAN technologies are used and information is often transmitted over the Internet, but various security mechanisms, such as Virtual Private Networks (VPNs), are usually used to protect against external users.

1.3- Ports and numbering

The network port is a software abstraction used to define the various endpoints of communication channels within a host. The network address, together with the port, identifies the endpoint of a communication channel within a network and is called a transport address (according to the OSI model). The sum of the network addresses and ports (one per host) of two communicating hosts uniquely identifies the communication channel between them and is called a network socket (or socket). Two hosts can have more than one communication channel with each other - in this case, the communication channels differ by at least one of their ports. The network port, in general, can be considered as a software analogy of the hardware port. In this analogy, the port can be seen as a point of contact between its communicating processes. The individual port of a host is identified by a number called the port number. This number is present in the message header of transport layer protocols. Such protocols are TCP, UDP. Computers can use up to 65,535 ports. Ports numbered 1 to 1023 are called well-known ports because they are standardized for specific services. Ports numbered 1024 to 49151 are available to be registered by software vendors to be used as identifiers between network endpoints for their applications. They must be registered with the Internet Assigned Numbers Authority (IANA). Numbers from 4915 2 to 65535 are called dynamic ports and are used at random.

1.4 - Network models

Network models describe best practices in computer networks. Their base is created watt network standards and specifications based on produced all networking products.

1.4.1 - OSI

OSI (Open Systems Interconnection Basic Reference Model) is a theoretical model describing the basic way of communication and the structure of telecommunication and computer networks. The so-called layers are used as the main building block - each layer provides an interface and services to the upper layer while receiving services from the layer below it. The OSI model provides a common framework for manufacturers and distributors to follow when designing hardware, operating systems, and protocols, defining standard specifications for communication between systems. The information sent over the network is in the form of data or data packets. And if two servers (A and B) wish to exchange information, the data from transmitter A must first be provided with official information about their transport and encapsulated (packed). The information moves from A to B, and when passing through the different systems, the data change due to the operation and functions of the individual levels (called layers). The receiving server B receives the data, where the processing of the information consists of the removal of the official information added for the purposes of transport at the sender.

The OSI model is conceptual and contains descriptions of the various functions and operations required for data exchange. These descriptions are logically grouped into separate stages (layers), as each layer contains similar in nature and design operations, a general presentation of the data, and has relative functional independence from the other layers. Although the practical implementation of network communications often violates these boundaries or unites neighboring layers, it always retains the logical sequence and dependencies. In each of the layers in the OSI model, except in the first and last, grouping (packing) of the data in portions is performed, during which two or more packets are formed. When packing, each layer adds its service information, such as sequence, error code, possibly addresses or service number, and other parameters depending on the required functionality at a given level. The process of transmitting and receiving information between the source and the receiver is carried out according to strictly defined rules, called a protocol. The protocol is a set of rules that determine the format of the data and the method of transmission and reception for the respective layer (transport is taken care of by the protocols from the lower levels, except for the channel level, where transport is difficult to define). Usually, the protocol does not affect more than one or two layers of the OSI model, ie. is designed for communication within the layer or between adjacent layers. This allows interoperability and portability of protocols in different transmission media (different implementations of the lower layers are allowed). The connection of protocols from different layers is done with the help of predefined interfaces, as each lower layer limits and determines the possibilities for transmitting information to the higher ones. During this process, the protocols from each layer exchange specific information/data called PDUs (Protocol Data Unit).

- Application layer

The Application Layer is the top layer of the OSI model, which applies to applications (programs) such as Internet browsers, remote management managers, messaging clients, HTTP, FTP, DNS servers, and others. This layer allows user applications to request services or information, and server applications to register and provide services on the network. Some of the main services that are registered on the application layer are e-mail, Web access, file and printer services (applications with network services), and others. Some of the more important protocols functioning on this layer are FTP, TFTP, DNS, HTTP, SMTP, Telnet, and others.

- Representative layer

The Presentation layer takes care of presenting the data in a form understandable to the recipient, providing their common format for different platforms. Performs data conversion and "translation", compression / decompression, as well as encryption / decryption of information. Representatives-related protocols include XDR, NFS, and others.

- Session layer

The Session layer controls the creation (and thus the interruption) of the sessions (dialogue) between the representative layers of two (or more) systems. It also controls the dialogue between two applications on different servers and manages data flows via checkpoints. This includes placing tags in the data stream. In case of incorrect transmission of the information or in case of termination of the connection in the network, the data should be transmitted only in their part after the last correctly transmitted token. The efficiency of flow control depends on the communication mode - full-duplex or half-duplex (in the first type both stations can "talk" at the same time, while in half-duplex at a time only one side can transmit data). A typical protocol operating in this layer is NetBIOS.

- Transport layer

The Transport layer provides end-to-end communication between processes running on different servers. Provides services with or without connection-oriented or connectionless services to the upper layers, depending on the protocols used. The layer uses client and server port addresses to identify different processes. Performs segmentation of the data submitted to it by the session layer, to properly arrange them by the recipient, determining a sequence number for each segment. Protocols related to the transport layer are TCP and UDP (the first - providing reliability, and the second - speed in data transfer).

- Network layer and

The main purpose of the Network layer is to set logical addresses of the source and destination, as well as to determine the best way to route the data. To achieve the best possible routing, the devices in the network layer (routers) use packet switching, which in short consists of reading the address of the logical destination received from one interface, the router sends the traffic (packets) via another interface to the destination. Protocols running on this layer are IP, IPsec, ICMP, IGMP, OSPF, and others.

- Channel layer

The channel layer (DataLink layer) aims to transmit and receive frames and is also responsible for their physical addressing. Before transmitting each package, a header (header) is added here - in the beginning - and a trailer (trailer) - at the end, thus turning it into a frame. Headers add network and transport layers to the data, but the trailer is only added at the Data-link level. The channel layer is divided into two sublayers, LLC and MAC, the former adding more control information for the proper transportation of data, and the latter provides access to the transmission medium (media). Some of the main characteristics of the layer are control of access to the transmission medium, the addition of hardware (MAC) addresses of the source and destination, preparation of packets for transmission (by encapsulating them in frames described above), calculation of the frame checksum (FCS) as well as the coding of electrical, light or electromagnetic pulses in the transmission medium. When transmitting data, sending devices to perform a residual cyclic check (CRC) or data sequence control (FCS) algorithm by recording the value obtained in the frame trailer. The receiving station executes the same algorithm and verifies the values, thus determining whether the frame was damaged during transmission. Protocols such as Frame Relay, ISDN, HDLC, PPP, etc. belong to this layer.

·   Physical layer

The Physical Layer is the lowest layer of the model and works only with ones and zeros (bits) that make up the frame. Its main function is to transmit bits over a communication line. The bits are coded as physical states of the transmission medium. In the case of wired cables, these are electrical signals, in the case of optical fibers - light pulses, and in the case of wireless connections - electromagnetic waves. In this layer, the electrical and mechanical characteristics that determine the presentation and formation of signals are important. This layer has specifications for the different types of transmission media and connectors, such as shape, structure, and composition.

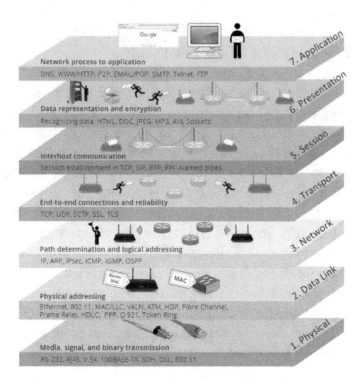

Figure 1 - OSI model

1.4.2 - TCP / IP

TCP / IP (Transmission Control Protocol / Internet Protocol) or Internet Protocol Suite is a conceptual model of a family of protocols for communication between computers, which is used on the Internet and in almost all other modern computer networks. This model consists of many protocols, but since the TCP and IP protocols play a key role, the name is determined by them. The TCP / IP model was created in 1980 because of the need for a single way to communicate between computers, thus enabling networks to be interconnected. In the TCP / IP model, the information is transmitted in the form of packets. Each package consists of 2 parts - header and data. It is often referred to as the Internet model, and in the early years of the Internet and the DoD model, as the development of the network model was funded by DARPA, an agency of the United States Department of Defense.

The TCP / IP model consists of protocols that are grouped based on their purpose into 4 "layers":

❖ Application layer

❖ Transport layer

❖ Network layer (Network / Internet layer)

❖ Channel layer (Physical layer)

In essence, the TCP / IP communication protocol package is the practical application of the OSI abstraction model. So we can compare the layers of the TCP / IP model with the layers of the OSI model.

The TCP / IP model has the following layers:

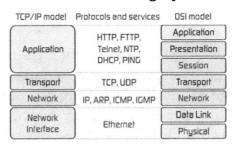

Figure 2 - TCP / IP

1.5 - Classification of networks

Networks are classified according to the following main characteristics:

. physical range;

. method of administration;

- network operating system;
- network protocols;
- topology;
- architecture.

We will consider only some of the above classifications.

1.5.1- Classification according to physical scope

Physical coverage should be understood as the size of the geographical area in which the network is located and, secondly, the number of computers in it.

According to their physical scope, networks are:

- local area networks (LAN - Local Area Network);
- city networks (MAN - Metropolitan Area Network);
- global networks (WAN - Wide Area Network).

The LAN covers a limited geographical area, such as a room, floor, or building. The number of computers in different LANs could vary significantly, starting from one or two computers at home or in the office and reaching tens or even hundreds of computers located in one building or many near each other.

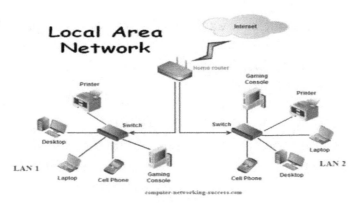

Figure 3 - Example of a LAN network

MAN networks are made up of two or more LANs located within a city (in an area with a radius of no more than 50 to 80 km). In scope, they occupy an intermediate position between LAN and WAN and are often classified as LAN or WAN instead of MAN. Therefore, the definition of MAN is rare. WAN covers wide geographical areas (more cities, countries, and even continents) and is made up of interconnected local area networks. The best example of a WAN is the global Internet. It is a set of computer networks of different types and topologies, which are interconnected and can communicate with the help of specially developed interface protocols (standards), which unite them in a common indistinguishable whole. But a WAN can also be a private network covering the local area networks of a company s offices whose branches are located in different cities or countries. Such WANs are also called the Internet. Unlike the global Internet, the term is written in lower case. When Internet technologies are used in a private WAN network, the network is defined as an extranet. WANs are subdivided into distributed and centralized. Distributed ones, such as the Internet, do not have a central control point, while centralized ones have a central server (for example, at the company's headquarters) to which all other computers are connected WANs are routed networks

This means that packets exchanged between LANs pass through gateways. The gateway is usually a router, which performs the routing functions. WANs can use private or public communication environments.WAN connections (connections between LAN networks) could be permanent or temporary, which are built during communication. Temporary relationships are more than a hundred common. WAN connections are generally slower than LAN connections.

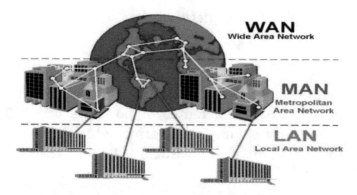

Figure 4 - Example of WAN / MAN / LAN

1.6- What is a VLAN?

Virtual Local Area Network (VLAN) is a method of dividing a physical computer network into different virtual networks for the purpose of the logical organization, control, and protection. Users in a VLAN can only communicate with each other, but not with users from other virtual networks. The advantage is that the same switches can provide multiple VLANs, thus saving equipment costs. As an example, we can consider a network of a company with three departments, located on three floors - Engineering, Marketing, and Accounting. The company has a physical

LAN that is used by all departments, but each department is separated into its own VLAN. The different ports of the switches are configured to provide access to the different VLANs. The employees of the Marketing Department on the first and second floors can reach each other and have access to their server, but they cannot access the servers and employees of the other two departments. If VLANs are not used, it will be necessary to build three separate physical networks - one for each department, which would make the solution at least three times more expensive.

CHAPTER II. NETWORK HARDWARE

2.1- Network interface cards

The Network Interface Card (NIC), also called a network adapter is a physical device. The drivers for it make the connection between the card and the operating system. They work in the channel layer of the OSI model. The network card converts the signal format from parallel to serial (serial). Units and zeros are converted into electrical pulses, light pulses, radio waves, or infrared rays. An important component of network cards is the transceiver, called a transceiver (transceiver). As its name suggests, it transmits and receives signals. In modern computers, Ethernet devices are integrated into the motherboard. Most often they are two b swarm at desktops and several laptops. Usually three transmission speeds are provided - 10, 100 and 1000 Mbps, corresponding to 10BaseT, 100BaseT and 1000 BaseT, respectively. The connection to the network is made using RJ- 45 type connectors and a UTP cable (unshielded in a twisted pair).

2.2- Router

The router is a stand-alone device that serves to control the distribution of traffic (packets) of information between different networks. To determine the path for data transmission and packet routing, the router uses a routing table that stores the IP addresses of other routers. This table is created by the router itself, obtaining information, and in case of any change, it updates it, "asking" the other routers who is connected to where. The routing table contains information about which networks it is connected to and how to send packets to them. Routers have a memory in which to store the routing table. It determines the source and destination of the packets. Routers are smarter devices than the switch and hub - they can choose the best route to an address from a variety of possible paths.

2.3- Switch

The main purpose of a switch is to choose a path to send data from the source to its destination in a given local network. The switch works with MAC addresses - this is a unique address on the computer's network card. The switch has a built-in memory. This memory is used as an intermediate connector between the sending and receiving computers. It stores the MAC addresses of the computers that are connected to the switch. When a computer sends a signal, it also contains the recipient's address. The switch checks in its memory the address for which the signal is intended and sends it only to the required port. Ethernet switches combine in one device the functions of two older Ethernet devices - the hub and the bridge: they connect several network components, as the hub does; manage traffic between systems to prevent conflicts, similar to bridge operation. Unlike the hub, the switch does not send the signal to all computers, but only to the computer for which the signal is intended. Therefore, it can correctly distribute data (signals) sent simultaneously from several computers without jamming other computers with unnecessary data, as the hub does. Unlike the bridge, which can transmit frames between only one pair of ports at a time, the switch supports data flow between all its ports at the same time. Most switches support full-duplex operations (simultaneous recep-

tion and transmission of information). Switches also centralize
the cable system.

CHAPTER III. IOT

3.1-What is the Internet of Things?

The Internet of Things (IoT) or Internet of Things is a concept of a computer network of physical objects (devices, vehicles, buildings, and other objects and things) having built-in electronic devices for interacting with each other or with the external environment. This concept considers the organization of such networks as a phenomenon capable of reshaping economic and social processes to exclude the need for human participation in part of actions and operations. The concept was formulated in 1999 as an extension of the application of radio frequency identification (RFID) in the interaction of physical objects with each other and with the environment. Since the 2010s, the concept of the Internet of Things has been filled with diverse technological content and new practical solutions have been introduced, and it is considered an upward trend in information technology primarily due to the ubiquity of wireless networks, the emergence of cloud computing the development of technologies for machine-to-machine interaction, the beginning of the active transition to IPv6 and the acquisition of software-configurable networks.

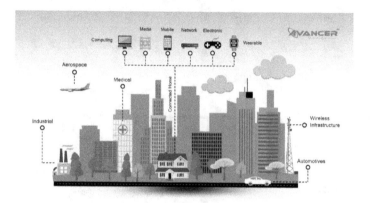

Figure 5 - Internet of Things (IoT)

3.2- History

The concept and term for it were first formulated by Kevin Ashton, founder of the Auto-ID research group at the Massachusetts Institute of Technology, in 1999 at a presentation to Procter & Gamble management. The presentation talked about how the comprehensive implementation of radiofrequency markers can change the management systems of logistics chains in a corporation. In 2004, Scientific American published an extensive article on the "Internet of Things", clearly demonstrating the possibilities of the concept in everyday life: it was demonstrated how household appliances (alarm clock, air conditioning), home systems (for garden watering, security, for lighting control), sensors (thermal, lighting and motion) and items (eg medicines with an identification marker) can interact with each other and ensure fully automatic processes (turn on the coffee machine, adjust the lighting, remind taking medicines, maintain the temperature, provide regular watering of the garden, save electricity). Various communication networks (infrared, wireless, power, and low-current networks) are used for this purpose. The home automation variants presented are not new in themselves, but the publication focuses on the integration of devices and objects into a single computer network served by Internet protocols and the consideration of the "Internet of Things" as a special phenomenon. In a 2008 report by the US National Intelligence Council, the Internet of Things was listed as one of the six potentially destructive technologies because of the ubiquitous and unobtrusive use of such common items as packaging by Internet users. goods, furniture, paper documents may pose a risk to national information security. Cisco analysts consider the period 2008-2009 to be the "real birth" of the Internet of Things, as they estimate that it is during this time that the number of devices connected to the global network has exceeded the population of the Earth, whereby the "human internet" has become the "internet of things". Since 2009, with the support of the European Commission, an Internet of Things conference has been held annually in Brussels, presenting reports from EU Commissioners and MEPs, government officials, executives of large companies such as SAP AG, SAS Institute Telefónica, leading scientists. Since the beginning of 2010 "internet of things" becomes the driving force of paradigm 'calculated ments in the mist "(fog computing), extending the principles of cloud computing centers for data processing to the huge number of interacting and geographically distributed devices which are seen as his platform. Since 2011, Gartner has placed the "Internet of Things" in the general maturity cycle of new technologies at the "technology trigger" stage, with an implementation period of more than 10 years, and in 2012 a special maturity cycle was created for technologies from The Internet of Things.

3.3-The technological point of view

3.3.1-Means of identification

The inclusion in the "Internet of Things" of objects in the physical world that are not necessarily equipped with an interface for connection to data transmission networks requires the application of object identification technologies ("objects"). Although the initial impetus for the emergence of the concept gives RFID technology, for this purpose can be used all means used for automatic identification: optically recognizable identifiers (barcodes, Data Matrix, QR codes), RTLS (means of determining the location in real mode time). With the widespread use of the Internet of Things, it is generally necessary to ensure the uniqueness of object identifiers, which in turn requires standardization. For sites directly connected to the Internet, the traditional identifier - the MAC address of the network adapter, allows the device to be identified at the channel level, and the range of available addresses is virtually inexhaustible (2^{48} addresses in the space of MAC-48), also, the use of the identifier at the channel level is not very convenient to implement. Wider opportunities for identification of such devices are provided by the IPv6 protocol, providing unique addresses at the network level for not less than 300 million devices per inhabitant of the Earth.

3.3.2-Measuring instruments

A special role in the Internet of Things is played by the means of measurement, ensuring the conversion of the data of the external environment into machine-readable data, at the same time filling the computing environment with significant information. A wide range of measuring instruments is used, from elementary sensors (eg temperature, pressure, illuminance), consumption meters (eg smart meters) to complex integrated measuring systems. Within the concept of the Internet of Things, measuring instruments are generally grouped into networks (eg wireless sensor networks, measuring systems), making it possible to build systems for inter-machine interaction.

A special practical problem in the implementation of the "Internet of Things" is the need to ensure maximum autonomy of the measuring instruments, above all to solve the problem of power supply to the sensors. Finding effective solutions that provide autonomous power supply to the sensors (use of photocells, conversion of vibration energy, air currents, use of wireless power transmission) will allow us to expand the sensor networks without increasing maintenance costs (eg for battery replacement or recharging of sensor batteries).

3.3.3-Means of data transmission

The range of possible data transmission technologies covers all possible means of wireless and wired (computer) networks. For wireless data transmission, such qualities as efficiency at low speeds, fault tolerance, adaptability, and ability to self-organize play a particularly important role in building the Internet of Things. Of major interest in this context is the IEEE 802.15.4 standard, which separates the physical layer and access control and which is the basis for such protocols as ZigBee, WirelessHart, MiWi, 6LoWPAN. Among the wired technologies, PLC plays an important role in entering the "Internet of Things" - technologies that allow the construction of data transmission networks over power lines, as many applications provide access to power supply networks (eg, vending machines, ATMs). , smart meters, lighting controllers are initially connected to the mains). 6LoWPAN, implementing the IPv6 layer over both IEEE 802.15.4 and PLC, being an open protocol standardized by the IETF, is noted as particularly important for the development of the "Internet of Things".

CHAPTER IV. THREATS AND MEASURES TO PROTECT NETWORKS AND SYSTEMS

4.1 - Introduction

We are at a fascinating moment in the evolution of what we now call the cyber defense. Mass data loss, intellectual property theft, theft of credit cards, identity theft, for timid about our integrity, denial of service (denial of service) - they have become a way of life for all of us in cyberspace.

Today, we have access to an extraordinary range of security tools and technologies, security standards, training, certifications, vulnerability databases, guidelines, best practices, catalogs of security controls, and countless security checklists, criteria, and recommendations. To help us understand the threat, we have seen the emergence of threat information channels, reports, tools, alarm services, standards, and threat sharing frameworks. In the beginning, everything is surrounded by security requirements, risk management frameworks, compliance regimes, regulatory mandates, etc. There is no shortage of information for security practitioners on what they need to do to secure their infrastructure.

4.1.1- Vulnerabilities and attacks

The vulnerability is a vulnerability or defect of the system. A vulnerability exists when there is at least one working attack or exploit. To secure a computer system, it is important to understand the attacks that can be made against it. These threats can be classified into one of the following main categories.

- "Back doors"

A "back door" in computer systems is any cryptosystem or algorithm that secretly bypasses normal controls for authentication or security. They can exist for a variety of reasons. They can be added by the authorized party to allow legal access or by an attacker for malicious reasons, but regardless of the reasons for their existence, they are a prerequisite for vulnerability.

- Denial-of-service attacks

DoS attacks are designed to make a machine or network resource inaccessible to users. Attackers can stop serving individual victims, such as by deliberately entering the wrong password enough consecutive times to block the victim, or they can overload one machine or network and block all users at once. While a network attack from a single IP address can be blocked by adding a new rule to the firewall, many forms of Distributed Denial of Service (DDoS) attacks are possible when the attack comes from a large number of points. Such attacks may originate from Botnet's zombie computers, but several other techniques are possible.

·   Attacks with direct access

An unauthorized user who gains physical access to a computer is often able to download data directly from it. It can compromise security by making operational changes to the system, installing software worms, keyloggers, or covert listening devices. Even when the system is protected by standard security measures, it can run another operating system or tool from a CD-ROM or other bootable media. Disk Encryption and Trusted Platform Modules are designed to prevent these attacks.

·   Eavesdropping

Eavesdropping is the act of secretly listening to a private conversation, usually between hosts on a network. For example, programs such as Carnivore and NarusInsight are used by the FBI and the National Security Agency to eavesdrop on ISP systems. Even machines that operate as a closed system (ie, without contact with the outside world) can be eavesdropped on by monitoring the electromagnetic fields generated by the hardware; TEMPEST is a specification from the NSA relating to these attacks.

·   Spoofing

Spoofing is a technique in which one person or program successfully impersonates another by falsifying data.

- "Violation of integrity"

Malicious product modification. The so-called "Evil Maid" attacks and security surveillance services in routers are an example of them.

- "Escalation of privileges"

Privilege escalation describes a situation in which a hacker with some level of restricted access can elevate his privileges or level of access without permission. For example, a standard user computer may be able to trick the system, giving access to limited data or even full unlimited access to the system.

- Phishing

Phishing is the attempt to obtain sensitive information such as usernames, passwords, and credit card information directly from users. Phishing is usually done through email phishing or instant messaging, and it often directs users to enter data into a fake website whose appearance and feel are almost identical to the real thing.

- Clickjacking

Clickjacking is a malicious technique in which a fake user attacker intercepts a button or link to another web page and redirects it. This is done using multiple transparent or opaque layers. The attacker basically "hijacks" the clicks intended for the top-level page and their route to another page, most likely owned by someone else. Careful drafting is a combination of styles, built-in frames, buttons, and text boxes, the user can be made to believe that he enters a password or other information in an authentic web page, while it is directed to an invisible frame controlled by the attacker.

4.1.2- Systems that are subject to hacker attacks

- Financial systems

Websites that accept credit card numbers and bank accounts are prominent targets for hacker attacks, due to the possibility of immediate financial gain from transferring money, making purchases, or selling information on the black market.

- Industrial equipment

Computers control the functions of many utilities, including the coordination of telecommunications, the power grid, nuclear power plants, and the opening of valves and the closure of water and gas networks. The Internet is a potential attack for such machines if they are connected to it. but the Stuxnet worm has shown that even equipment controlled by a computer that is not connected to the Internet can be vulnerable. In 2014, an emergency computer protection team, a unit of the Ministry of Internal Security, investigated 79 hacker incidents in energy companies.

- Aviation

The aviation industry is highly dependent on a series of complex systems that can be attacked. A simple power outage at an airport can cause repercussions throughout the world, most of the systems rely on the radio that could be interrupted and controlled. It would be especially dangerous for aircraft over the oceans because radar surveillance extends only 175 to 225 miles on the high seas. There is also the potential for the attack within aircraft. The consequences of a successful attack range from loss of confidentiality to loss of system integrity, which can lead to more serious problems and, such as disruptions to the network and air traffic control, which in turn can lead to airport closures, loss of aircraft, loss of life of passengers, damage to land and transport infrastructure. A successful attack on the military aviation system that controls ammunition could have even more serious consequences.

- Consumer devices

Desktops and laptops are often infected with malware to collect passwords, financial account information, or to build a botnet to attack other targets. Smartphones, tablets, smartwatches, and other mobile devices have also become targets and many have sensors, such as cameras, microphones, GPS receivers, compasses, and accelerometers, that could be used to collect personal information. including sensitive health information. WIFI, Bluetooth, and cellular telephone networks can be used as triggers for an attack. Home automation tools like the Nest thermostat are also potential targets

- Large corporations

Large corporations are a common target. In many cases, this is aimed at financial gain through identity theft and involves data breaches, such as the loss of millions of customer credit card data from Home Depot, Staples, and Target Corporation. However, not all attacks are financially motivated, for example, the security company HBGary Federal suffered a serious series of attacks in 2011 by hacktivist PUP Anonymous. Sony Pictures was attacked in 2014.

- Cars

If the car's internal (local) rail is accessed, it is possible to disengage the brakes or turn the steering wheel. Computerized control of individual engine units, cruise control, anti-lock brakes, seat belt pretensioners, door locks, airbags, and modern driver assistance systems or even self-driving cars make these interventions possible and even go even further. . Modern cars now use WiFi and Bluetooth to communicate with users' portable devices, as well as the mobile phone network - to connect to a doorman or emergency services or to receive navigation or entertainment information. Each of these networks is a potential entry point for malware with an offensive or hacker attack. Researchers in 2011 was even able to use a malicious CD in the car's stereo system as a successful pretext for an attack. Vehicles with built-in voice recognition or remote on-board assistance are equipped with microphones that could be used for eavesdropping.

In a 2015 report, US Senator Edward Markey criticized manufacturers' safety measures as inadequate and also stressed that information on driving style, vehicle location, and diagnostic data of the engine and chassis of the car can be easily collected, which is a high risk of abuse by both manufacturers and hackers.

. Government

The government and military computer systems are often attacked by activists as well as foreign forces. Local and regional authorities, traffic control, police, intelligence these units, records of personnel, and financial systems are also potential targets as they are now largely computerized.

4.1.3- Damage from security breaches

Serious financial damage was caused by security breaches, but as there is no standard model for calculating accident damage, the only data are those published by the affected organizations. Several security consulting firms are estimating the total global losses caused by viruses, worms, and hostile digital acts. Estimates of losses in 2003 range from $ 13 billion (from worms and viruses alone) to $ 226 billion (for all forms of covert attacks). However, a reasonable estimate of the financial cost of violations of the security can help organizations to make rational investment decisions.

4.1.4- Motives for attack

As with physical security, motivations for computer security breaches vary between attackers. Some are thrill-seekers or vandals, others are activists or criminals seeking financial gain. State-sponsored attackers are common and well-informed.

A standard part of the threat model for each specific system is to determine what can motivate an attack on that system and who might be motivated to do so. The level and specificity of precautions vary depending on the system. Home PC, banking, and secret military network, all face very different threats, even when the underlying technologies that are used are similar.

4.1.5- Computer protection (countermeasures)

In computer security, a countermeasure is an action, device, procedure, or technique that reduces a threat and vulnerability. Some common countermeasures are:

· Security measures

A state of computer "security" is conceptually ideal, achieved through the use of three processes: prevention, detection, and response. These processes are based on various policies and system components, which include the following:

User account access and cryptography can protect files and data systems.

Firewalls are currently the most common prevention systems in terms of network security, as they can (if properly configured) prevent access to internal network services, as well as block certain types of attacks by packet filtering. Firewalls can be both hardware and software-based.

Intrusion Detection Systems (IDS) are designed to detect network attacks.

The 'response' is necessarily determined by the assessed security requirements for an individual system and can cover the range of simple protection upgrades, notification to legal authorities, counter-attacks, and the lie In some special cases, the complete destruction of the compromised system is preferred, as not all compromised resources may be detected

Today, computer security consists mainly of "preventive" measures, such as firewalls. A firewall can be defined as a way to filter network data between a host or network and another network, such as the Internet, and can be applied as device software by hooking up to the network stack to provide real-time filtering. time and blocking. Another embodiment is the so-called physical firewall, which consists of a separate machine filtering of network traffic. Firewalls are common between machines that are permanently connected to the Internet.

However, relatively few organizations maintain computer systems with efficient detection systems, and even fewer have organized on-site response mechanisms. As a result, Reuters points out: "Companies lose more through electronic data theft than physical theft of assets." The main obstacle to the effective eradication of cybercrime can be traced to over-reliance on firewalls and other automated systems. This is the basic gathering of evidence - by using packet- grabbing devices that put criminals behind bars.

· Vulnerability reduction

However, that formal verification of correctness of computer systems is possible, it is not yet common.

Cryptography, properly implemented e hardly possible to drill directly.

Two-factor authentication is a method of reducing unauthorized access to the system or sensitive information. It requires "something you know"; password or PIN, and "something you have"; card, dongle, cell phone, or other pieces of hardware. This increases security because unauthorized this person will need both to get access.

Social engineering and attacks with direct access to the computer (physically) can only be prevented by non-computer means, which can be difficult to implement, in terms of information sensitivity. Even in a very disciplined environment, such as in military organizations, attacks can still be difficult to predict and prevent.

It is possible to reduce the chances of an attacker by constantly updating the systems with the help of a security scanner and / or hiring competent people who are also responsible for security.

· Security through design

Design security or alternatively project security means that software is designed from the beginning to be secure. In this case, certainly so is considered a major feature.

Some of the techniques of this approach include:

The principle of least privileges, where each part of the system has only the privileges that are necessary for its function. Thus, even when the attacker gains access to this part, he has only limited access to the entire system.

Automated theorem, trying to prove the correctness of crucial software subsystems.

Code reviews and single tests approach to make modules more secure when formal evidence is not possible.

Defense in depth, when the structure is such that more than one subsystem must be violated violates the integrity of the system and the information it possesses.

Full disclosure of all vulnerabilities to ensure that the " vulnerability window " is maintained as short as possible when bugs are detected.

- Security architecture

Open Architecture Security defines IT security architecture as 'artifact design ', which describes how security controls (security countermeasures) are positioned and how they relate to the entire information technology structure. These checks aim to ensure the quality of system attributes: confidentiality, integrity, availability, parity, and service provision.

Technopedia defines the security structure as "a single security design that meets the needs and potential risks associated with a particular scenario. It also specifies when and where to apply security controls. The design process is usually reproducible.

- Hardware protection mechanisms

USB dongles typically used in schemes for software licensing unlock software options, but they can also be a way to prevent unauthorized access to a computer or other device software. The dongle, or key, essentially creates a secure encrypted tunnel between the software application and the key. The principle is that a receiver encryption scheme such as the Advanced Encryption Standard (AES) provides a stronger security measure.

Another application security for them is to use them to access web-based content such as cloud software or virtual private networks (VPN networks). Also, USB dongles can be configured to lock or unlock workstations.

Disabling USB ports is a security option to prevent unauthorized access to a secure computer. Infected USB dongles connected in a network with a computer inside the firewall are considered by Network World as the most common hardware of threat to the computer they networks.

Access to mobile devices is increasingly secure, as ordinary passwords are not sufficiently secure and are gradually being replaced by biometric scanning features. Eye, face, and fingerprint identification are about to replace current regular passwords.

- Secure operating systems

Companies invest a lot of time, effort, and resources in protecting their systems, and some even set up operational security centers. They use firewalls and anti-virus tools, but they also spend a lot of time monitoring networks and looking for anomalies that may be an indication of a breach.

Windows - the popular choice

The security issue can also be reformulated: Will the company is more secure if it abandons Microsoft Windows? To say that Windows dominates the corporate market is to underestimate the situation. NetMarketShare found that 88% of all computers on the Internet use a version of Windows.

Microsoft continues to improve security on Windows systems. This includes rewriting the operating system's codebase adding its own antivirus software system, improving firewalls, and implementing sandbox architectures where programs cannot access the operating system's memory or other applications.

But the popularity of Windows is a problem in itself. The security of the operating system can depend largely on the size of its installation base. This is what the creators of malware (Malware) are looking for According to some experts, Windows will always rank last among operating systems in terms of security precisely because of the large number of users. There is no doubt that from Melissa to WannaCry - much of the malware is directed against Windows systems.

macOS and security through the unknown

If the most popular operating system will always be the main target of hackers, then using a lesser-known one would not be safer? This idea is similar to the concept of "security through the unknown", in which internal software developments are kept secret as the best way to protect against attacks.

Although macOS is considered a completely secure operating system with a system with few vulnerabilities, it should be borne in mind that in recent years, hackers have not ignored the Mac universe. Experts point out that the system is relatively secure so far, but this is mainly due to the "security through the unknown" approach and the fact that Microsoft is a much more attractive target.

However, experts agree that Linux is the most secure operating system at the moment. But while companies often choose it as a server operating system, very few organizations use it on their employees' computers.

Here, however, companies have to make another choice - which Linux system to choose - and this complicates the decision a little more. Users will probably want a user interface that looks a little more familiar; while managers will above all insist on the most secure operating system.

The main important difference with other operating systems is that Linux is open-source. The fact that coders can read and comment on each other's work seems like a security nightmare. But this is becoming an important reason why Linux is such a secure operating system. Anyone can review the code and fix bugs or leaks. The very fact that hundreds and sometimes thousands of people have scanned each line of code minimizes the possibility of finding vulnerabilities.

Another factor for greater Linux security is a better user rights model. Windows users have administrator access by default, which means that almost everything in the system is open to them, while Linux has far greater restrictions.

. Access control capabilities and lists

Checklist access (Access control list, abbreviated ACL) in telecommunication networks means a list of access control. An ACL is a set of rules that specify what restrictions to impose on traffic passing through a device. Typically, ACLs are placed on a device port, choosing which traffic passing through the port restricts the access control list - inbound or outbound. Different device manufacturers use different ACL writing formats. The network administrator can enter the ACL through the command line, or it can be entered through a web interface.

For example, the following ACL is in Cisco format:

permit TCP host 10.0.0.2 any eq 80

deny IP host 10.0.0.2 192.168.0.0 0.0.0.255

permit ip any any

An ACL is applied to the port input of a router. The rules apply from top to bottom. The first line allows the device with IP address 10.0.0.2 to access TCP port 80 at random addresses. The second line prohibits the access of the device with address 10.0.0.2 to network 192.168.0.0/24. The third row allows any other traffic.

4.2 - Management of authorized and unauthorized devices

It needs active management (inventory, tracking, and correction) of all hardware devices on the network in order to provide access only to authorized these devices and prohibit unauthorized devices to gain access to a resource.

Why is this control important?

Attackers, located all over the world, are constantly scanning the address space of target organizations waiting to join the network of new and unprotected systems. Attackers can take advantage of new hardware that has just been installed on the network but is not configured and protected with appropriate security updates Even devices that are not visible from the Internet can be used by attackers who have already gained internal access. Additional systems that connect to the enterprise network (eg demonstration systems, temporary test systems, wireless / wired guest networks) must also be carefully isolated to prevent negative access to the security of information systems. of the given enterprise

With BYOD (Bring your own device) - where employees bring personal devices to work and connect them to the corporate network - these days often common principle. These devices can now be compromised and used to infect internal resources.

It needs active management (monitoring, reporting, and correction) configuration for the security of laptops, servers, and workstations using a rigorous process of configuration management and change control to prevent the use of vulnerable services and settings from the attackers.

Figure 6 - Security control

4.3 - Intrusion Detection System (IDS)

An intrusion detection system (IDS) is a type of software that is designed to automatically notify administrators when an entity outside of an IT infrastructure attempts to gain unauthorized access to information through malicious activity or security breaches.

IDS works by tracking activity tracking and exploring weaknesses in a system, checking file integrity, and conducting analysis that looks for a behavioral pattern of already known attacks. In addition, IDS automatically searches the Internet to update definitions of the latest threats that could lead to future attacks.

There are several ways that IDS uses to detect threats. In **signature-based detection, the** model or signatures are compared to previous cases of intrusion detection and threats. This technique is used to detect already known threats, as well as their variations or hidden threats

Another type of attack detection is detection based on anomalies in systems and networks - the definitions predefined by an administrator are compared, according to which the normal functioning of the system is determined with the current ones and if the specified limit is exceeded, the characteristic " abnormal " is set. and appropriate measures are taken.

IDS combines or is part of a larger security system that also includes firewalls, antivirus software, and more. NIDS is trying to detect malicious actions such as denial-of-service attacks, port scanning, and network traffic monitoring attacks.

4.3.1- There are three main components of IDS

NIDS - Network Intrusion Detection System - analyzes the traffic of a network by comparing the current data flow with parameters of already described or prevented attacks, which are stored in databases.

NIDS reads all incoming packets and searches for suspicious models. When threats are detected based on their severity, the system can take action such as notifying administrators or blocking network access to the source's IP address.

Penetration detection systems (IDS) are available in different types; The two main types are the host-based penetration system (HBIS) and the network-based penetration system (NBIS). In addition, there are IDSs that also detect movements by looking for specific markers of well-known threats.

(NNIDS): This is similar to NIDS and only one specific host on the network is monitored, not an entire subnet.

Host Intrusion Detection System (HIDS): This takes a "picture" of the file system of the entire system and compares it to a previous picture. If there are significant differences, such as missing files, the system alerts the administrator.

Intrusion Detection System (NIDS) is used to monitor and analyze network traffic to protect the system from network threats.

4.4- Intrusion Prevention System (IPS)

Intrusion Prevention System (IPS) is a system that monitors a network for malicious actions such as security threats or policy violations.. The main function of the IPS is to identify the suspicious activity and then register information, try to block the activity, and finally report it.

Systems for preventing penetration are also known as systems for detecting and preventing penetrates not (IDPs).

IPS can be implemented as a hardware device or software. Ideally (or theoretically) IPS is based on the simple principle that " dirty " traffic enters and " clean " traffic exits.

A network intrusion prevention system (NIPS) is a system used to monitor a network, as well as to protect the privacy, integrity, and availability of a network. Its main features include protecting the network from threats, such as denial-of-service (DoS) attacks and unauthorized use of resources.

NIPS monitors the network for malicious activity or suspicious traffic by analyzing protocol activity. Once NIPS is installed on a network, it is used to create physical protection zones. This in turn makes the network intelligent and quickly recognizes good traffic from bad traffic. In other words, NIPS becomes a prison for hostile traffickings, such as Trojans, worms, viruses, and polymorphic threats.

The intrusion prevention system (IPS) is located online and monitors traffic. When a suspicious event occurs, he takes action based on certain prescribed rules. An IPS is an active real-time device as opposed to a non-embedded intrusion detection system that is a passive device. IPS is considered to be the evolution of the intrusion detection system.

NIPS are manufactured using high-speed integrated circuits (ASICs) and network processors, which are used for high-speed network traffic, as they are designed to execute tens of thousands of instructions and comparisons in parallel, unlike a micropro- cessor that executes one instruction at a time.

Most of NIPSs use one of three methods for detection, as follows:

• Opening the basis of signature/signature/signature are pre- defined and pre-configured attacks. This detection method moni- tors network traffic and compares it to pre-configured signatures to find matches. If a match is found successfully, NIPS takes the following appropriate actions. This type of detection can not identify threats such as "zero-day".

• Anomaly detection: This detection method creates a baseline of average network conditions. After the baseline is created, the system periodically tests the network traffic based on statistical analysis and compares the sample with the created baseline. If the activity is found to be outside the baseline parameters, NIPS takes the necessary action.

• Protocol state change detection: This type of detection method identifies protocol state deviations by comparing the monitored events with predefined profiles.

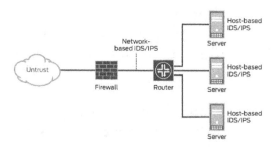

Figure 7 - IDS / IPS

4.5 - Continuous assessment of vulnerability

Security engineers must work in a constant flow of new information: software updates, fixes, security messages, threat bulletins, etc. Understanding and managing vulnerabilities have become an ongoing activity that requires significant time, attention, and resources.

Attackers have access to the same information and can take advantage of the gaps between the emergence of new knowledge and removal. For example, when those engineers who explore vulnerabilities reported new vulnerabilities, began competition among all countries, including the attackers (to be " ln weapons empowered " to attack tons); suppliers of software and hardware (to develop, to implement patches or under the sole and updates) and engineers in the security (to make a risk assessment, regression test adjustments installation).

Organizations that do not scan for vulnerabilities and proactively address identified vulnerabilities are likely to compromise computer systems.

Figure 8 - Risk assessment

4.6 - Control of administrative rights

Abuse of administrative rights is a key method for attackers to spread to the target enterprise. Two very common attack techniques take advantage of uncontrolled administrative privileges. First, a workstation user who works as a privileged user is tricked into opening a malicious email attachment, downloading and opening a file from a malicious website, or simply browsing a website that hosts attacking content that may automatically use browsers. The file or exploit contains executable code that is executed on the victim's machine either automatically or by deceiving the user who executes the attacker's contents. If the victim's user profile has administrative rights, the attacker can take full control of the victim's machine and install remote control software to find administrative passwords and other sensitive data. Similar attacks happen with email. The administrator inadvertently opens an email that contains an infected attachment, and it is used to retrieve information on the network that is used to attack other systems. The second common technique used by attackers is the brute force method of a user's administrator password to access the target machine. If administrator passwords are free and widely distributed, for example, identical to passwords used on less critical systems, the attacker has a much better chance of gaining full control of the systems.

4.7 - Maintenance, monitoring, and analysis of reports (Logs)

Deficiencies in security registration and analysis allow attackers to hide their location, malware, and activities they have performed. Even if the victims know that their systems have been compromised, without protected and complete records (Logs) they are blind to the details of the attack and the subsequent actions taken by the attackers. If there are no solid reports the attack may go unnoticed indefinitely and the specific damage may be irreversible.

Sometimes logs are the only evidence of a successful attack. Many organizations maintain audit records for compliance purposes, but attackers rely on the fact that such organizations rarely look at audit logs, so they do not know that their systems have been compromised. Due to poor or non-existent log analysis processes, attackers sometimes control the victims' machines for months or years without knowing anyone in the target organization, although evidence of the attack has been recorded in unverified logs. Most free and commercial operating systems, network services, and firewall technologies offer registration options. Such registration must be enabled by sending the log files to the centralized registration servers. Firewalls, proxies, and remote access systems (VPN, dial-up, etc.) must be configured for detailed logging, storing all available login information in case further investigation is required. In addition, operating systems, especially those on servers, must be configured to create access control logs when a user attempts to access resources without the appropriate privileges. It often takes human experience and intuition to identify and understand attack events though there is automated software designed for this purpose.

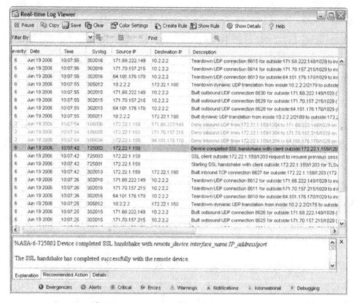

Figure 9 - Real-time report

4.8- Email and Web protection

Web browsers and email clients are often focused on attack due to their high technical complexity and flexibility, as well as their direct interaction with users and other systems and websites. Content may be designed to entice or mislead users to take actions that significantly increase the risk and allow the introduction of malicious code, loss of valuable data, and other attacks.

4.8.1-Web browser

Most web browsers today have basic security features, but it is not enough to rely on one aspect of security. The web server consists of layers that provide many opportunities for attack. The basis of any web browser is the operating system, and the secret to ensuring that it stays secure is simple: update it with the latest security patches. Make sure your patches are up to date and installed correctly, as any server running old patches will fall victim.

Update all software components that run on a web server. Anything that is not essential, such as DNS servers and remote administration tools such as VNC or Remote Desktop, should be disabled or removed. However, if remote administration tools are essential, avoid using easy passwords. This does not apply to remote access tools, but user accounts, switches, and routers.

A flexible firewall is one of the strongest forms of protection against security breaches. When targeting a web server, the attack will immediately attempt to upload hacking tools or malware to take advantage of the security breach before it is fixed. Without a good antivirus package, security breaches can go unnoticed for a significant period of time. Cybercriminals can exploit cookies in malicious ways. Changing your browser settings to block third-party cookies will reduce this risk. The autocomplete or autocomplete feature saves keystrokes by storing information you have recently entered. However, auto-completing login information is a big risk if your laptop is lost or stolen. And limiting supplements to an absolute minimum will reduce the chance of attacks. Add-ons can contain malware and increase the chances of your browser attacking. Configure your browsers to prevent them. Most popular browsers use a database of phishing and / or malware to protect against the most common threats. Make sure you and your users are protected. A pop-up blocker can be used. Pop-ups are not only annoying but can also directly contain embedded malware or entice users to click on something that uses social tricks. Make sure the browser of your choice has enabled pop-up blocking.

4.8.2-Email

Email is one of the best and interactive ways in which x plow work with computers, promoting proper behavior is just as important as technical settings.

Passwords containing common words or phrases, easy to " crack ". Make sure that strong passwords are created; the combination of letters, numbers, and special characters is complex enough. It is recommended that the passwords be changed regularly every 45-60 days.

Implementing two-factor authentication is another way to ensure that the user is authentic by reducing the attack surface. Using a spam filtering tool reduces the number of malicious emails that come into your network. Policies configured in the email client help to verify that the domain from which the emails come is authentic in order to reduce the receipt of spam and phishing. Install this tool encryption to protect emails and communications adds another layer to the user and network-based protection.

4.9-protection against malicious software (Malware)

Malware is an integral and dangerous aspect of Internet threats and can be designed to attack your systems, devices, or your data. It can move fast, change quickly, and enter several points such as end-user devices, email attachments, web pages, cloud services, user actions, and removable media. Modern malware can be created to evade defense or to attack or disable. The protection of malware has to be able to work in this dynamic environment through large-scale automation, fast updating, and integration processes such as response to incidents (Incident Response). They must also be located at several possible critical points in the systems to detect, stop, or monitor the execution of malware. Paquet Titeni protection systems of organizations provide administrative functions to verify that all the protections are active and up to date on each managed system.

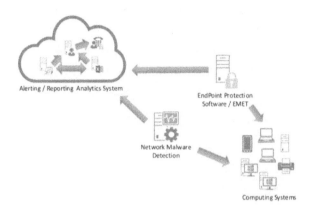

Figure 10 - Diagram of the relationship between system units for protection against malware

5.0-Restriction and control of network ports, protocols, and services

Attackers are looking for remotely accessible network services that are vulnerable to exploitation. The most common examples are poorly configured web servers, mail servers, file and print services, and DNS servers (Domain Name System) installed by default on different types of devices, often without a business need for a service. Many software packages automatically install services and include them as part of the installation of the underlying software without informing the user or administrator that the services are allowed. Attackers scan for such problems and try to exploit these services, often trying by default for user IDs and passwords or widely available exploitation code. Port scanning tools are used to determine which services are "listening" on the network for several target systems. Also, to which ports are open, efficient scanning software can be configured to identify the protocol version and " listen " to each open port detected. This list of services and their versions is compared with the inventory of services required by the organization for each server and workstation in an asset management system. Recently added features in this scanning software are used to detect changes in the services offered by scanned machines on the network since the previous scan, helping security personnel identify time differences.

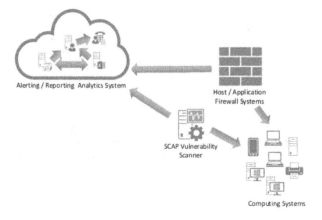

Figure 11 - Diagram of the relationship between system units regarding the restriction and control of network ports, protocols, and services

5.1-Ability to recover data

When attackers compromise machines, they often make significant changes to configurations and software. Sometimes they also make slight changes to the data stored on compromised machines, potentially compromising organizational efficiency with contaminated information. Once detected, for organizations that do not have a reliable data recovery capability, it can be extremely difficult to remove all aspects of a machine attacker's presence. Once a quarter (or when new spare equipment is purchased), the testing team must evaluate a random sample of system archives, trying to restore them to a test environment. Recovered systems must be checked to ensure that the operating system, application, and backup data are unchanged and functional.

In the event of a malicious infection, recovery procedures should use a version of the backup copy that is considered to precede the original infection.

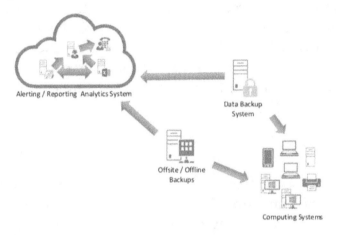

Figure 12 - Diagram of the relationship between system units regarding data recovery capabilities

5.2-Secure configurations for network devices such as firewalls, routers, and switches

As shipped by manufacturers and retailers, default configurations for network infrastructure devices are aimed at ease so of use rather than security. Open services and ports, default profiles or passwords, support for old (vulnerable) protocols, preinstallation of unnecessary software; all can be operated in their default state.

Attackers take advantage of less securely configured network devices over time, as users require exceptions for specific business needs. Sometimes exceptions are configured and then it is forgotten to remove them when they are no longer applicable to business needs. In some cases, the security risk of the exception is not properly analyzed or measured against the related business needs and may change over time. Attackers look for vulnerable default settings, electronic firewall holes, routers, and switches and use them to infiltrate security. They exploit flaws in these devices to gain access to networks, redirect traffic to the network, and capture information during transmission. Through such actions, the attacker gains access to sensitive data, changes important information, or even uses a compromised machine to present itself as another reliable system on the network.

5.2.1-Best practices for protection against this type of attack and

- Compare the firewall, router, and switch configuration to the standard secure configurations defined for each type of network device used in the organization. The security configuration of such devices must be documented, reviewed, and approved by the organization's change control board. Any deviations from the standard configuration or updates to the standard configuration must be documented and approved in a change management system.

- Any new configuration rules that go beyond the baseline that allows traffic to pass through network security devices, such as firewalls and network IPS, must be documented and recorded in a configuration management system, with a specific business reason for each change. . The name of the specific person responsible for this business need and the expected duration of the need.

- Use automated tools to check standard device configurations and detect changes. All changes to these files must be saved and automatically reported to security personnel.

- Manage network devices using two-factor authentication and encrypted sessions.

- Install the latest stable version of all security updates on all network devices.

- Network engineers can use a specially designed machine for all administrative tasks or tasks requiring increased access. This device must be isolated from the organization's core network and not have Internet access. This machine should not be used for reading emails, composing documents,s or surfing the Internet.

- Network infrastructure management through network connections that are separate from the business use of that network, relying on separate VLANs or, preferably, on completely different physical connectivity for network device management sessions.

5.2.2-Procedures and tools

Some organizations use commercial tools that evaluate a set of network filter device rules to determine whether they are consistent or in conflict, by providing automated checking for network filter problems and debugging rule sets or checklists. access (ACL) services through the device. Such tools must be run whenever significant changes to a firewall rule, routine ACLs, or other filtering technologies are made.

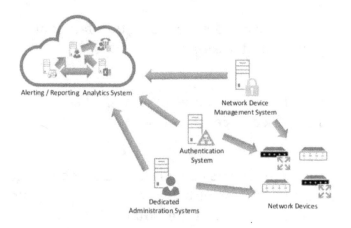

Figure 13 - A diagram of the relationship between system units on h Protecting configurations for the network they devices

5.3- Protection of borders

Attackers focus on using systems that can access the Internet, including not only demilitarized zones (DMZ) systems but also workstations and laptops that retrieve content from the Internet across the network. Threats such as organized crime groups and nation-states use configurational and architectural weaknesses found in perimeter systems, network devices, and client machines with Internet access to gain initial access to an organization. Then, with the base of operations of these machines, attackers often orient themselves to sneak deeper into the borders, to steal or change information, or to establish a permanent presence for later attacks on internal hosts. Also, many attacks occur between networks of business partners, sometimes called extranets, as attackers move from one organization's network to another, exploiting vulnerable extranet perimeter systems. To control the flow of traffic across network boundaries and police content by seeking attacks and evidence of compromised machines, border protection must be multi-layered, relying on firewalls, proxy servers, DMZ perimeter networks, and network IPS and IDS. It is also crucial to filter inbound and outbound traffic. It should be noted that the boundaries between internal and external networks are narrowing as a result of the increased interconnectivity within and between organizations, as well as the rapid growth of the deployment of wireless technologies. These blurry lines sometimes allow attackers to gain access within networks by bypassing border systems. However, even with this blurring of borders, effective security deployment still relies on carefully configured border protections that divide networks with different threat levels, user groups, and control levels. And despite the blurring of internal and external networks, effective multilayer perimeter defenses help reduce the number of successful attacks, allowing security personnel to focus on attackers who have created methods to circumvent border restrictions.

Figure 14 - Diagram of the relationship between system units regarding border protection

5.3.1-Procedures and tools

Additional recommendations here are aimed at improving the overall architecture and implementation of both the Internet and the internal border points of the network. The internal segmentation of the network is essential for this control because once within the network, many offenders try to focus on the most sensitive m ESTA. Typically, internal network security is not configured to protect against an internal attacker. Setting even a basic level of segmentation security of the network and protecting each segment with a proxy server and firewall will significantly reduce access intruder to other parts of the network. One element of this control can be accomplished by using free or commercial IDS and sniffers to search for attacks from external sources targeting DMZ and internal systems, as well as attacks originating from internal systems against DMZ or the Internet. Security personnel should regularly test these sensors by running vulnerability scan tools to verify that the scanner's traffic is triggering an appropriate signal. IDS sensor enclosures must be scanned automatically, using an automated script each day, to ensure that the log volumes are within the expected parameters and that the log files are properly formatted and have not been corrupted. Moreover, tracking software packages (sniffers) to be located in the demilitarized zone (DMZ), to look for traffic Hypertext Transfer Protocol (HTTP), which surrounds the HTTP proxy. By periodically sampling traffic, for example for three hours once a week, information security staff can search for HTTP traffic that is not provided or intended for a DMZ proxy, which means that the requirement to use a proxy server is circumvented.

5.4-Data protection

The data is in many places. The protection of this data is best achieved by applying a combination of encryption protection, integrity protection, and data loss prevention methods. As organizations continue their move towards cloud computing and mobile access, it is important to take appropriate care to limit and report data retrieval while mitigating the effects of compromising data. The adoption of data encryption, both in transit and at rest, provides mitigation of data compromises. This is true if care is taken in the processes and technologies associated with coding operations. An example of this is the management of cryptographic keys used by various algorithms that protect data. The process of generating, using, and destroying keys must be based on proven processes defined in standards such as NIST SP 800-57. It should also be taken, to ensure that products used in an enterprise, perform well-known and tested cryptographic algorithms identified by NIST. Reassessment of the algorithms and key sizes used in the enterprise on an annual basis is also recommended to ensure that organizations do not lag behind in the level of protection applied to their data. For organizations that move data to the cloud, it is important to understand the security controls applied to data in the middle of multiple cloud tenants and to determine the best course of action for implementing encryption and key security controls. Whenever possible, keys should be stored in secure containers, such as hardware protection modules (HSM). Encryption (encryption) data provides such a level of confidence that even if data is compromised, it is impossible to access to the texts to be found without significant resources, but must be created and controls to reduce the threat of data mining in the first place. Many attacks occur on the web, but others are carried out by physically stealing laptops and other equipment containing sensitive information. But in most cases, victims are unaware that sensitive data is leaving their systems because they are not monitoring outbound data flows. The movement of data across the network, both electronically and physically, must be carefully studied to minimize exposure of attackers. The loss of control over protected or sensitive data by organizations is a serious threat to business operations and a potential threat to national security. While some data is leaked or lost as a result of theft or espionage, most of these problems are the result of misunderstood data practices, lack of effective policy architectures, and user errors. Data Loss Prevention (DLP) refers to a comprehensive approach involving people, processes, and systems that identify, monitor,r, and protect the data used through in-depth content inspection and a centralized management framework. Over the past few years have seen a notable change in av attention and investment from securing the network to securing systems within the network and securing the data itself. DLP controls are rule-based and include the classification of sensitive data, the discovery of data in an enterprise, the application of control mechanisms, and reporting and auditing to ensure compliance with the rules.

Commercial tools are offered to support the enterprise management of encryption and key management in the enterprise and include the ability to support the implementation of encryption controls in the cloud and mobile environment.

The definition of life cycle processes and the roles and responsibilities associated with key management must be undertaken by each organization.

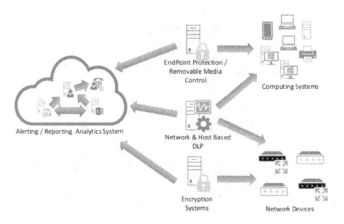

Figure 15 - Diagram of the relationship between system
units regarding data protection

5.5-Controlled access based on the need to know

Some organizations do not carefully identify and separate their most sensitive and critical assets from less sensitive publicly available information about their internal networks. In many environments, internal users have access to all or most critical assets. Sensitive assets may also include systems that provide management and control of physical systems (eg SCADA). Once attackers enter such a network, they can easily find and retrieve important information, cause physical damage, or disrupt low-resistance operations. For example, in several strong breaches reported in the last two years, attackers were able to gain access to sensitive data stored on the same servers with the same level of access as far less important data. There are also public examples of providing access to a corporate network to gain access and then control physical assets and cause damage.

It is important for the organization to understand what its sensitive information is, where it is located, and who needs access to it. To derive sensitivity levels, organizations need to compile a list of key data types and overall relevance to the organization. This analysis will be used to create a common data classification scheme for the organization. At the basic level, the data classification scheme is divided into two levels: public (unclassified) and private (classified). Once personal information is identified, it can be further subdivided based on the impact it would have on the organization if it were compromised. Once the sensitivity of the data has been established, the data must be traced back to the business applications and the physical servers that host those applications. The network must then be segmented so that systems with the same level of sensitivity are on the same network and are segmented by systems with different levels of trust. If possible, firewalls should control access to each segment. If the data is distributed on a network with a lower level of trust, encryption must be used. Performance requirements must be established for each user group to determine what information the group must have access to perform its tasks. Based on the requirements, access should only be granted to the segments or servers that are required for each task. Detailed logging should be enabled for all servers to track access and investigate situations where someone has access to data they should not have.

5.6-Access control in wireless networks

Major data thefts have been initiated by attackers who have gained wireless access to organizations outside the physical building, bypassing the security perimeter of organizations by connecting wirelessly to access points in the organization.

Wireless customers accompanying traveling employees become regularly infected through remote operation while traveling or in Internet cafes. Because they do not require direct physical connections, wireless devices are a convenient reason for attackers to maintain long-term access to the target environment. Effective organizations use commercial wireless IDS scanners to detect intrusion.

Furthermore, the security team should periodically capture wireless traffic from the boundaries of a facility and use the free and commercial tools for analysis to determine whether the wireless traffic was betrayed by weaker protocols or crypts injured than organization it e. When devices based on weak wireless security settings are identified, they must be found in the organization's asset inventory and reconfigured more securely or have limited access to the organizational network.

Also, the security team must use remote control tools on the wired network to retrieve information about wireless capabilities and devices associated with managed systems.

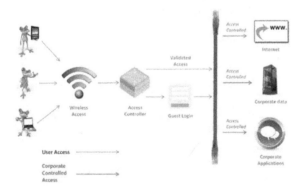

Figure 16 - Control access to wireless these networks

5.7-Monitoring and control of accounts

Attackers often find and exploit legitimate but inactive

user profiles to impersonate legitimate users, making it difficult for network observers to detect attackers' behavior. For example, some malicious insiders or former employees may have access to the accounts left in the system s long after a certain period while keeping its access to the system so the organization's sensitive data for unauthorized and sometimes malicious purposes. Although most operating systems include options for logging account usage information, these features are sometimes disabled by default. Even when such features are present and active, they often do not provide details for accessing the default system. Security officers can configure systems to record more detailed account access information and use third-party scripts or analysis tools to analyze that information and user access to user profiles on different systems. Profiles also need to be tracked very carefully. Each passive profile must be deactivated and possibly removed from the system. All active accounts must be tracked back to authorized users of the system and it must be ensured that their passwords are stable and changed regularly. Users must also log out of the system after a period of inactivity to minimize the possibility of an attacker using the system retrieving information from the organization.

Figure 17 - Diagram of the relationship between system

units regarding Monitoring and control of accounts

5.8-Protection of software applications

Attacks often take advantage of vulnerabilities found in web-based and other application software. Vulnerabilities can occur for many reasons, including coding errors, logical errors, incomplete requirements, and failure to test for unusual or unexpected conditions. Examples of specific errors include the inability to verify the amount of user data; inability to filter unnecessary but potentially malicious sequences of input streams; inability to initialize and clear variables; and poor memory management, which allows flaws in one part of the software to affect unrelated (and more important for security) parts. There is a flood of public and private information about such vulnerabilities, available to both attackers and defenders Attackers can inject specific exploits, including buffer overflows, SQL injection attacks, page-to-page scripts, fake inter-page queries, and code clicks to gain control of vulnerable machines. In one attack, more than 1 million web servers were exploited and turned into engines to infect visitors to these sites using SQL injection. During this attack, reliable websites by government governments and other organizations compromised by attackers were used to infect hundreds of thousands of browsers that accessed those websites. Numerous vulnerabilities in web and non-web applications are detected regularly.

Application security (internally developed or acquired) is a complex activity that requires a complete program covering the entire policy, technology, and role of people. They are often broadly defined or required by formal risk management frameworks and processes.

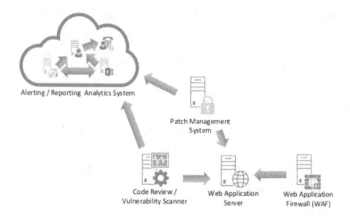

Figure 18 - Diagram of the relationship between system units regarding the protection of software applications

5.9-Management and response to accidents

Cyber incidents are now part of our way of life. Even large, well-funded, and technically sophisticated companies struggle to cope with the frequency and complexity of attacks. The question of a successful cyber-attack on a company is not "if", but "when".

When it happens accident is too late to develop proper procedures, reporting, data collection, management responsibility, legal protocols, and communication strategy, which will enable the company to successfully understand and manage to recover. Without an incident response plan, the organization may not detect an attack in the first place, or if the attack is detected, the organization may not follow good procedures to limit damage, eradicate the attacker's presence, and recover safely. In this way, an attacker can have a much greater impact, causing more damage, infecting more systems, and possibly retrieving more sensitive data than would be possible if there was an effective incident response plan.

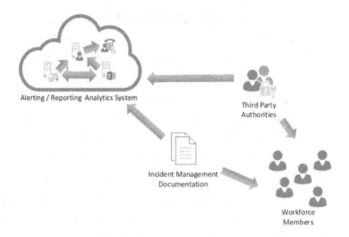

Figure 19 - Diagram of the relationship between system units regarding incident management

After defining detailed incident response procedures, the incident response team should engage in periodic scenario-based training, working through a range of attack scenarios, fine-tuned with the threats and vulnerabilities faced by the organization. These scenarios help ensure that team members understand their role in the incident response team and also help them prepare for dealing with incidents.

6.0-Penetration tests

Attackers often take advantage of the gap between good defense projects and intentions and execution of maintenance. Examples include the time window between declaring a vulnerability, the presence of a patch from the manufacturer, and the actual installation of each machine; well-intentioned policies that do not have an implementation mechanism (especially those designed to limit risky human actions); non-application of good configurations and other practices for the whole enterprise or machines entering or leaving the network; and a misunderstanding of the interaction between multiple security tools or normal system operations that have security implications. Also, successful protection requires a comprehensive program of technical protection, good policy and governance, and appropriate human action. In a complex environment where technology is constantly evolving and new attackers are regularly appearing, organizations must periodically test their defenses to detect gaps and assess their readiness. Penetration tests begin with the identification and assessment of vulnerabilities that can be identified in the enterprise. It complements this by designing and conducting tests that specifically demonstrate how the adversary can either undermine the organization's security objectives (eg, the protection of a specific intellectual property) or achieve specific objectives (eg, establishing a hidden management infrastructure and control). The result provides more in-depth insight by demonstrating the business risks of various vulnerabilities. Penetration tests provide significant value, only when already in place basic security measures when they are executed as part of comprehensive ongoing program management and improve security. They are often defined and required by formal risk management frameworks and processes. Each organization should define a clear scope and rules for commitment to penetration testing. The scope of these projects must include at least systems with the highest value of the organization and functionality for product processing. Other lower value systems can also be tested to see if they can be used as reference points for compromising higher-value targets. Penetration test engagement rules should describe at least the hours of the day of testing, the duration of the tests, and the overall approach to testing.

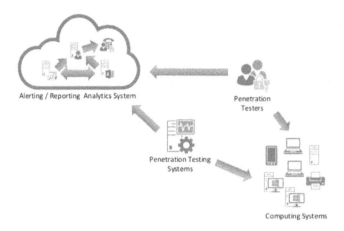

Figure 20 - Diagram of the relationship between system units regarding penetration tests

Conclusion

In a period of the rapid development of network and information technologies, on the one hand, the pursuit of new services and the improvement of our well-known voice information on the other hand and achieving the integration of these services in a supportive environment is a challenge for IT and networking professionals. branch.

The high level of development is due to the growing dependence of the economy and the market on these technologies. It is important for the corporation to maintain its economic condition at a high level, and this is impossible without maintaining the appropriate level of the management process, and it is related to the supporting IT and network technologies.

Therefore, we can conclude that:

- The future in building networks to maintain integrated services is in building "gateways" to integrate these services;
- This would lead to the use of a single supporting transmission medium (IP networks), which facilitates the management of the system;

- Reduction or reduction of part of the costs for maintenance and management of the network and its services;
- Increasing the security of both the transmitted information and the services in the network.